PLANTS & FLOWERS AS ORNAMENT

CD-ROM & BOOK

Th. M. M. van Grieken

DOVER PUBLICATIONS, INC.
Mineola, New York

The CD-ROM in this book contains all of the images. There is no installation necessary. Just insert the CD into your computer and call the images into your favorite software (refer to the documentation with your software for further instructions). Each image has been saved in both 72-dpi Internet-ready and 300-dpi high-resolution JPEG formats.

The "Images" folder on the CD contains two different folders. All of the high-resolution JPEG files have been placed in one folder and all of the Internet-ready JPEG files can be found in the other folder. The images in each of these folders are identical. Every image has a unique file name in the following format: xxx.JPG. The first 3 digits of the file name, before the period, correspond to the number printed under the image in the book. The last 3 letters of the file name "JPG," refer to the file format. So, 001.JPG would be the first file in the JPEG folder.

Also included on the CD-ROM is Dover Design Manager, a simple graphics editing program for Windows that will allow you to view, print, crop, and rotate the images.

For technical support, contact:
 Telephone: 1 (617) 249-0245
 Fax: 1 (617) 249-0245
 Email: dover@artimaging.com
 Internet: **http://www.dovertechsupport.com**
 The fastest way to receive technical support is via email or the Internet.

Copyright

Copyright © 2009 by Dover Publications, Inc.
Electronic images copyright © 2009 by Dover Publications, Inc.
All rights reserved.

Bibliographical Note

Plants & Flowers as Ornament CD-ROM and Book, first published by Dover Publications, Inc., in 2009, contains all of the images from *De Plant in hare Ornamentale Behandling,* originally published by J. H. van de Weijer, Groningen, in 1888.

Dover Electronic Clip Art®

These images belong to the Dover Electronic Clip Art Series. You may use them for graphics and crafts applications, free and without special permission, provided that you include no more than ten in the same publication or project. For permission for additional use, please write to Permissions Department, Dover Publications, Inc., 31 East 2nd Street, Mineola, New York 11501, or email us at rights@doverpublications.com

However, republication or reproduction of any illustration by any other graphic service, whether it be in a book, electronic, or in any other design resource, is strictly prohibited.

International Standard Book Number
ISBN-13: 978-0-486-99035-4
ISBN-10: 0-486-99035-4

Manufactured in the United States by Courier Corporation
99035402
www.doverpublications.com

Note

This collection of ornamental plant forms is from a rare, nineteenth-century portfolio by Dutch artist Th. M. M. van Grieken, who was often compared to Owen Jones. These exquisite chromolithographs were originally used as reference tools for artists, architects, and designers. Displaying over 300 botanical forms, including buds, blooms, entire plants, leaves, Art Nouveau designs, and more, this exquisite collection continues to be a source of inspiration.

de
PLANT
in hare
ORNAMENTALE
BEHANDELING
D·O·O·R
Th. M. M. van GRIEKEN.

met eene Inleiding:
„over de
Zinnebeeldige Voorstelling,"

2 Titelplaten, 38 Albumplaten,
4 tekstplaten en 150 tekstfiguren.
—

Chromo-Lith. en Uitgave
van de Firma J. H. v. d. WEIJER
GRONINGEN.

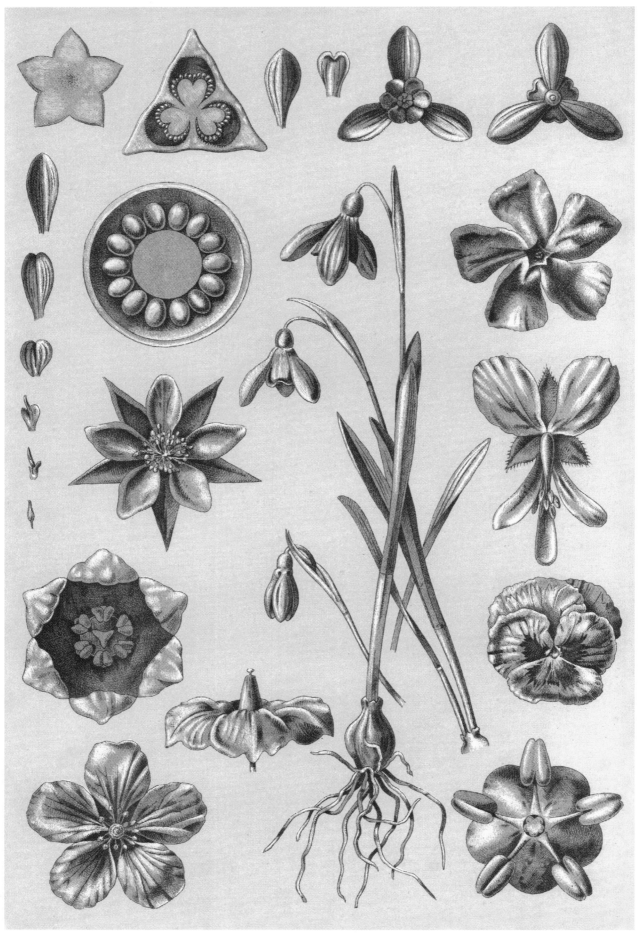

10 060–068

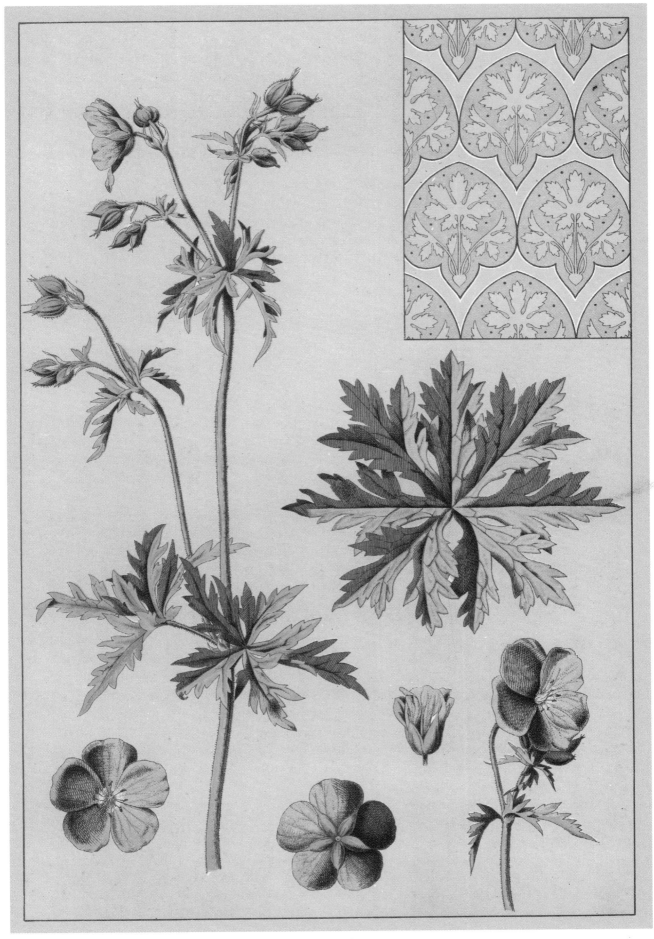

073–079

080–087

088–095

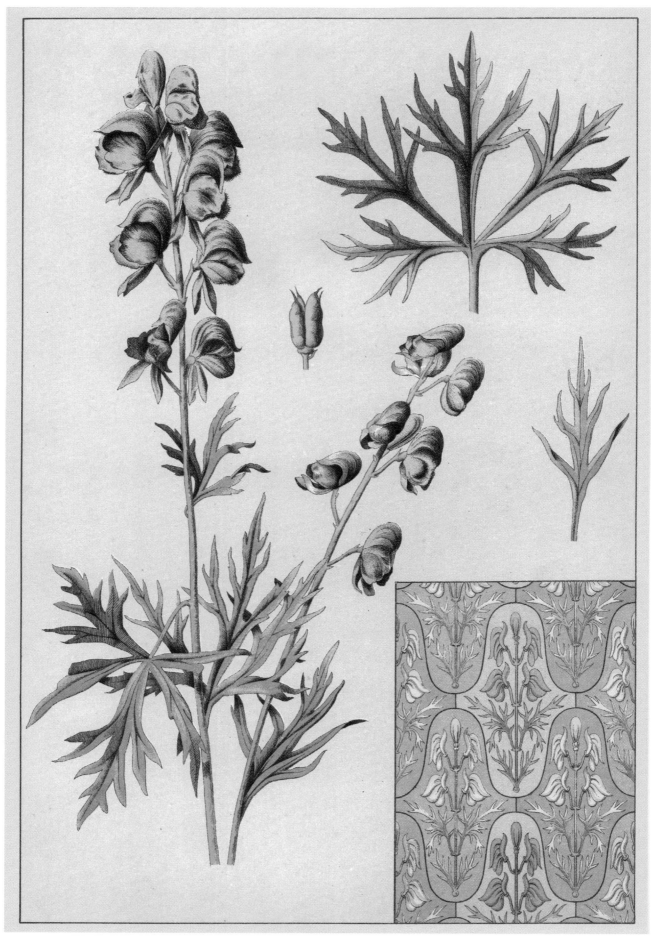

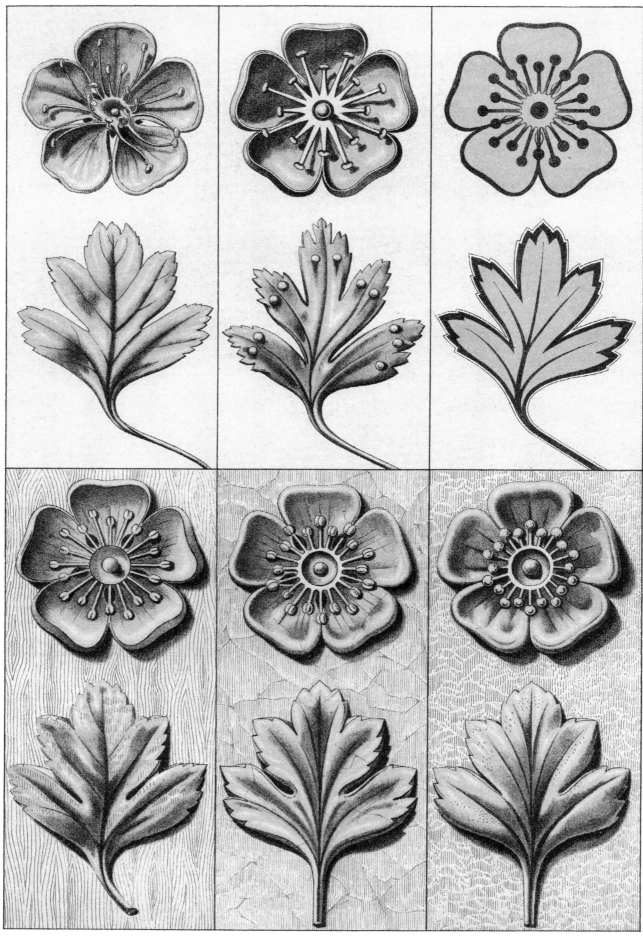

112–128

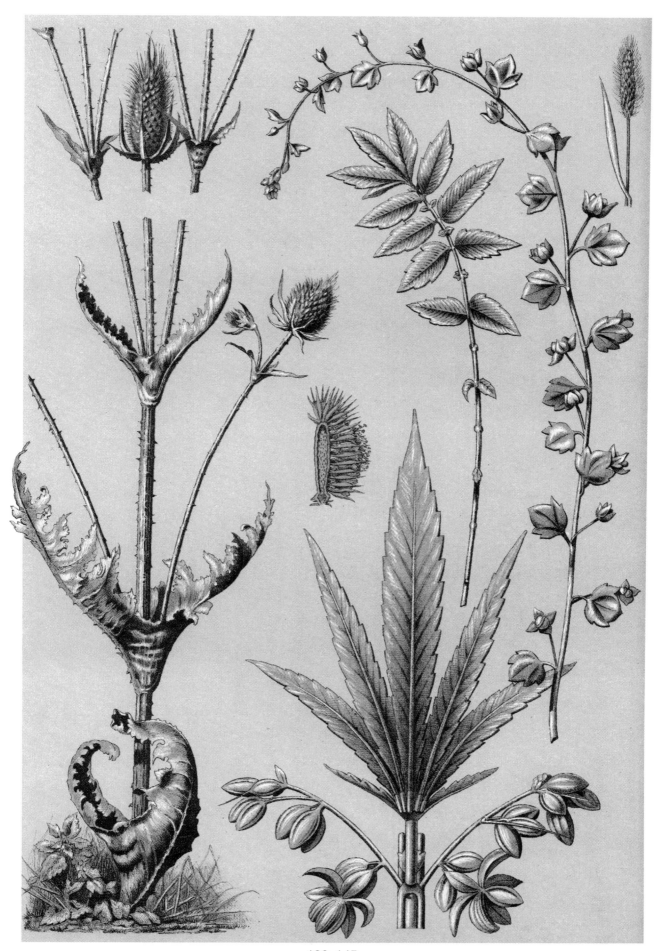

139–145

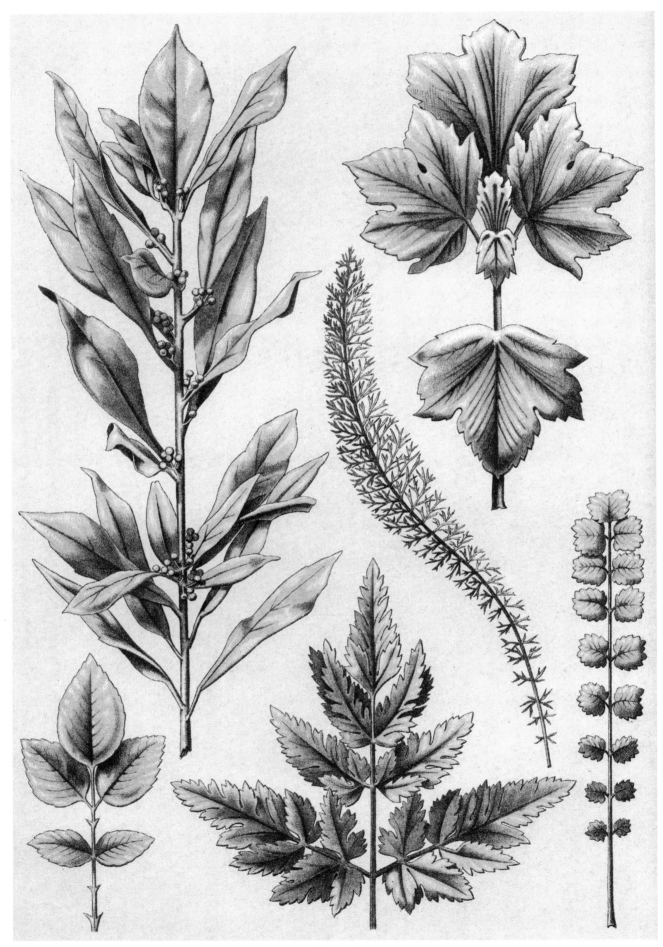

152–159

168–175

176–187

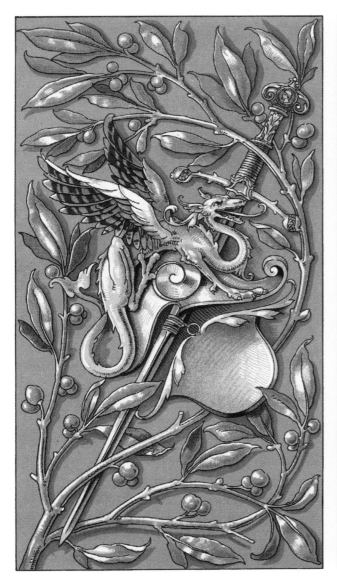

188–190

PALMÆ

28

191–200

201–202

203–208

KROKUS.
NARCIS.
TULP.

209–210

211–229

233–241

ROOS.

40   271–274

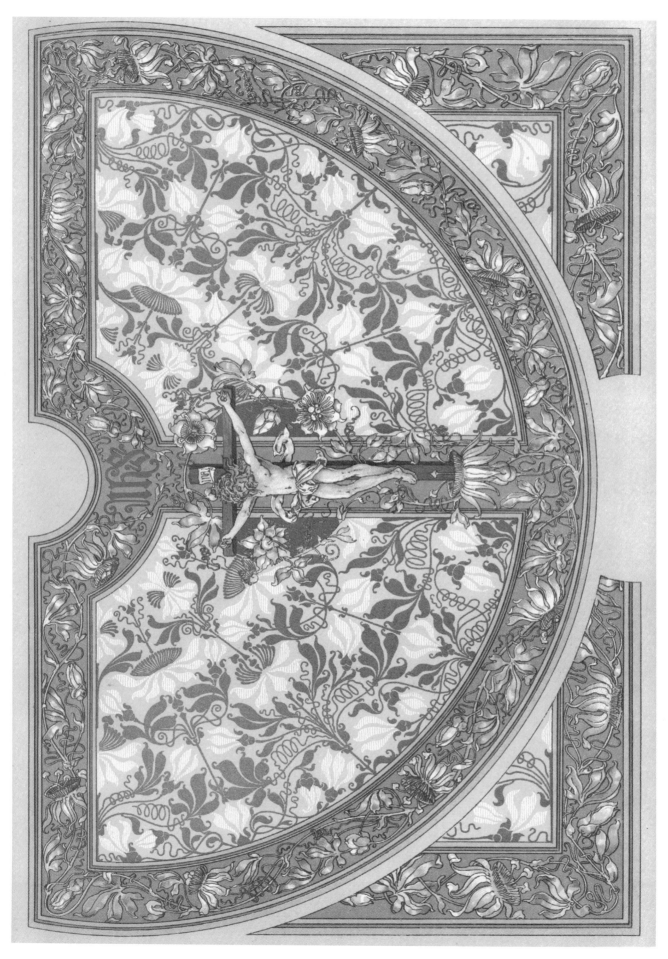

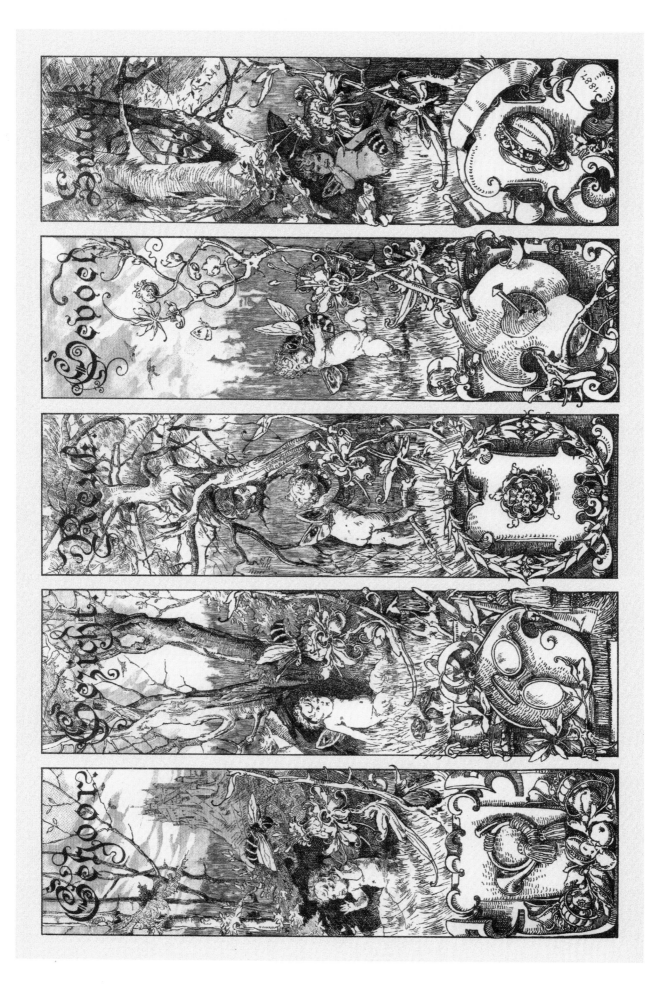

287–291

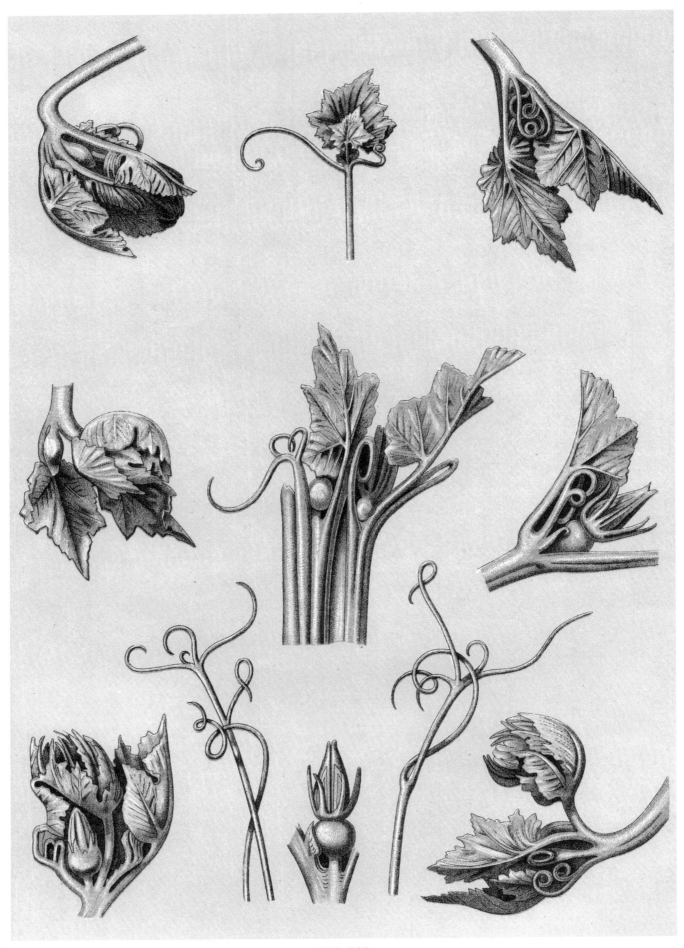

292–302

303